LEAVING THE NINETY-NINE

When Love found Me

Dr. ANNU JOHN

BookLeaf Publishing
India | USA | UK

Made with ❤ on the BookLeaf Publishing Platform
www.bookleafpub.in
www.bookleafpub.com

Dedication

To every soul searching for Light,
To every heart longing for Love.

Preface

A shepherd had one hundred sheep. When one of them went astray, he left the 99 searching for that lost one. And when he found it, he didn't punish it yet lifted it up in his arms. Will you go to such lengths just for that 'one' who wandered away?

I've experienced love in many forms - through family, relationships, friendships. But in the long run, I realized that all were conditional; the way they loved me and the way I loved them back, all came with expectations.

But then I met someone who loved me unconditionally. A love that held me close when I drifted away. Even when I messed up and was to difficult to forgive, it didn't abandon me. It came searching for me. A love that left the ninety-nine just to find me!.

This book is a collection of poems that talk about this love. And if you are someone who feels unworthy or unseen, may this book remind you that you are still being sought, held and loved by a Love that has no conditions and never lets go.

Acknowledgements

"Trust in the Lord with all your heart and lean not on your own understanding;
In all your ways acknowledge Him, and He shall direct your paths." Proverbs 3:5-6

I thank the Lord Almighty for His grace and guidance. Though I have written in different genres since childhood, when He said, "Write for Me," everything changed — and it has been great ever since.

To my husband, Jeffin — you are the best thing that has ever happened to me, and every other blessing unfolds from there.

To my sisters, Sarah and Maria, who have been my most honest critics and constant encouragers.

To my parents, who appreciated everything I wrote since childhood — even when some of it was truly terrible.

To my brothers and nephews, thank you for patiently enduring my pestering and for reading whatever I placed in your hands.

To my parents-in-law and my soul sister Sandra, thank you for your support in publishing this book, and for making me feel truly part of the family.

And to everyone who has been part of my life's journey – I owe you big hugs.

1. When Love Found Me!

Darkness was my friend, so was despair
Loneliness had its hold on me
The world seemed useless, so did humans
It was hard to find a reason to live.

Longed for care, yet none offered
Called myself unworthy of Love
Weary on those streets I walked
Envying people who loved each other.

Then I heard Him, calling my name
Drawing nearer and holding me closer
Showed me His love, led me to the cross
Where He ached through His nailed hands.

That was Love, that died for my past
Bore my sins till He bled to death
Saved me from eternal curse,
The Love that gave me a new life.

Gave me peace I'd longed since ever
Keeping me secure in His arms
Assured me that I'm not forgotten
But worth dying for, that I was loved by one.

That's Jesus, who saw me at my worst
Yet gave me a purpose to live for,
Gave His life without asking, hence
Now I know I've one to Love.

2. Unconditional Love

Oh God, enthroned above all
How humble of You to come down
And give away Your life for me
So that I regained my life.

This spiritual life
This joy of eternity
This love of You
All these are Unconditional

You didn't deny pouring out
Even Your last drop
I can't believe that this greatest sacrifice
Was for a worse sinner like me!

You refused all your fame and positions
And all that You had in your Father
Just for the sake of my sin
That I won't be dead by it

I should have seen myself burned
Scorned in the wrath of God
But You didn't allow that to happen
You stretched Your hands and gave up Your life.

How cannot I call this love
Unconditional, yet it's more
More than mine or anyone's words
To describe the depth of Your Love!

3. The Unworthy Me!

I ask You: Lord ,what You saw in me?
For calling me to do Your will
For choosing me for Your purpose
When I am meek and lowly

I know not where this ends
On the final day when I'm before You
Will I really have the sheaves in my hands
That are saved from the other side?

For I have not the courage
Neither the skills
To share Your word to the world
Nor am I holy and perfect

With every temptation, I fall
With every sin, I fail
Reached the verge of giving up
Still You never give up on me!

Oh! Your mercy has covered me
Picked me up and made me stand
Led me to the rock that is higher than I
Gave me second last chances

So when I ask: Why me?
You reply: Because it is I,
The Lord your God, so never fear
For I am with thee till the end.

4. CONFIDENCE

When I look at myself
At my imperfections
The sins I hold on
The talents I never have

I've nothing to boast about
Not even a bit of goodness
Nothing to keep me going
No belief in myself.

But when I look at God
How can I comprehend?
That among all the people,
He chose me too?

The God who never makes mistakes,
If He saw my laziness
Yet chose me for His glory
Aren't I worth it?

If He knows my potential
To be used for His kingdom
Isn't that my confidence,
Not in self but in God?

So when I remember His promises
And abide in them with faith
Why should I withhold my confidence
When God has full confidence in me?

5. You, not me!

I don't know what to write for You
I want to bring You a sonnet,
A worship song, A poem;
Anything that is meaningful
Anything that gives you glory.
Anything that draws others to You.

'Cause you are the Eternal, the Mighty,
The only true God who saved us
Who gave His life to redeem us
A closest friend and wonderful teacher
Who created the snows,
The lilies, and the flamingos!

How can I stop, How can I hold myself?
If this pen and paper is all I have
To use it for You, to write for You
How can I deny it when You're all I have
The only hope to live on earth
The only thing that keeps me moving.

Though I'm fragile, though I am unworthy
Though my art is unpolished,
Though I fail and though I stumble,

Though my faith waver at the slightest fear
Yet I know it's about You
And not in the least about me.

'Cause prisons shake at your words
Your presence fills rooms of worship
When one or two are gathered for You
Your grace overwhelms their plans
For it's You and ultimately You
And never who or where all do.

So when I come to You as an offering
When doubts overshadow my faith
When I focus only on my sins,
Help me to remind that it's You, not me
You with open arms, embrace whatever I give
As my loving and all comforting Father!

6. The Choice

When now I wander through the woods
Embracing the lilies, and touching the leaves
I look upon the silver rivers and ponder
Upon my reflection, upon my life.

Amidst whatever happened around,
It was an elevator of choices.
From choosing between candies, to between toys,
To choosing between friends, and opting a career,
My whole life was mended by
Choices of people and passion.

As a child, I chose whatever I wanted
As an adult, I chose upon people's pressure.
Jubilance did it weave, so did melancholy
Hard days weren't far to find
Mysteries written from days of old
Black and white were its hue.

But, as the elevator moved on,
No longer people influenced me.
It's God who guides my path
Not necessity, nor the society
Trusting the Lord with all my heart

And not leaning on mine own understanding.

Looking back, I find myself evolved
As a perfect plan by the great architect
Who moulded me and walked with me
And joined my broken pieces.

And when God, time and life
Took a 'U turn', to return back,
To my dandelions of childhood,
Blew to spread its colorful wings,
Soared higher up to the skies
Where the Mighty and just God
Heed to the dreams I longed.

7. Worship

All the claps and shouts
Whisper in my ears
Each with a song of praise
Each breath carrying His name
Each mouth shouting aloud
"Our God is mighty"
Yes what a Mighty God we have!

It's more than these loud voices
It's more than the words of millions
Even all of these praises
Are not enough to worship Your glory!

Still we know You look at us
You won't count our deeds futile
You won't turn a blind eye
To the little things that we offer
For Your name to be exalted.

And that's why we are glad
To call our God Awesome
To be happy at nothing else
Yes what a Mighty God we have!

8. Long Awaited Paradise

(Personifying the people of Israel when they were delivered out of slavery from Egypt.)

Far far from dust, dirt and dryness
Far from the arid dry patches of land
From sin, slain of the wicked,
Tribulations, trials and troubles.

We, the uncountable multitude of people
The chosen ones by God
Each man, woman and child
Redeemed by the blood of the Lamb.

Are busy, packing trunks
To set out to a new adventure
Escaped from the fire of slavery
To a new ray of hope and peace.

We are no longer a slave to Pharaoh
No longer far from God
The destroyer has fled from us
And all our tears have been wiped.

'Cause our Lord, the holy God of Israel

Has chosen us to be His nation
No longer can any plagues strike us
For His promised land is nearer.

The land of honey and milk
The land of prosperity and peace
Blue hills, calm rivers
Birds, flowers and all wonders of nature.

Though the Red Sea rises against us
We see Pharaoh's armies drowning
A long way of dry land prepared for us
That leads to our promised land.

Yes, we see that promised land
Before us, beyond the waters
We see our long awaited freedom
Prepared for us- God's people.

9. Bride

Adorned in precious jewels of gold
Bearing crowns of glistening emerald
Clothed in majestic white linen
Petals of lily embellishing her hair

Her eyes sparkle like the stars
Her smile captures the entire hall
Her walk resembles that of a bride
Waiting for her dear one

There she waits, for her man
To tramp the doorsteps of her mansion
And come and take her to His land
Where she will be His forevermore.

Her gold was the faith she had in Him
That moved mountains of sorrow in her life
The Crown of Life was that she earned
For enduring till her last breath.

Sweat and blood had she perspired
When she fought the good fight.
The linen reflects her righteous acts
Deeds of leading a holy life

Not defiled by worldly dirt
White as snow is it's hue.

Behind her elegance lies the days
Of trial, toil & hardships of old
Happiness hadn't met her eyes
Till the present day-her big day!

Where she waits, longing for her groom
To draw near and hold her hand
And take her to His home
Where they would begin Chapter One
Of a new story, of the life she waited,
Beyond the seas, between the clouds,
Embracing the heavens...

10. One Man

(Personifying the woman caught for adultery, whom Jesus forgave.)

Those few years seemed like decades
For decades had I been in darkness
Burned in sin, dipped in sorrow
Slave to the evil pleasures of this world
Making my body and soul impure.

But, when I got caught,
Became a laughing stock of society,
I cried out loud, yet none heard me
All those who were partakers of my past,
Mocked me to their hearts' content.

And now, in the dust
Cursing myself and this life
Without anyone to wipe my tears,
Heed my cry, or bear my sins
There I laid, stoned almost to death.

One hand, that wrote on the sand
One mouth that spoke out wisdom
One pair of eyes that looked with empathy

One hand that stretched out to me
One mouth which spoke: "Never sin again"

That one person who saved me
My sins were washed within a second!
A new soul breathed unto me
And I, breaking the chains of sins,
Was set free, was forgiven!

By that One Great Man
Who died on the cross for my sins
The blood that flowed through His feet
Redeemed me to a new life
A new life of joy and peace.

Oh, how that darkness changed to light
How that sorrow changed to hope
How my impurity turned to sanctity
By that one Man, the Greatest,
The King of Kings, and Lord of Lords..

11. Waiting

(Personifying one of the members of the church of Corinth.)

"Paul is coming to our church next week."

"Really? What a pleasant news!"

What joy filled my heart
When I heard that good news
Now I can go and make
All the preparations done:
Clean my church,
Clean the room for him to stay
Make delicious food to serve
Set apart tithes to give
Oh, what joy fills my heart
Musing his arrival!

It's far more than waiting for my family
More than waiting for my friends,
Or waiting for a bridegroom;
'Cause it's the arrival of someone
Who showed the way to save my life!

Saved my life from fire
Saved my life from wrath
Saved my life from eternal hell.

Gone are the days of sorrow
Gone are the days of sin
'Cause when that one day
Paul came and preached the gospel
About Christ who died for my sins
And I was saved and baptized in His name.

Oh, what peace ruled my heart
What joy like never before!
All my sins were forgiven
And a life Eternal granted free!

Oh, now when I read his letters
To our church, the Corinthians
I'm happy at his joy about us
Yet also heed his advices
And this joy of waiting for him
To hear him preach again and again.

Still, it's not more than another waiting
For the day my Lord Jesus returns
When our life on Earth will finally end,

And we will inherit a new home,
Prepared for us, His everlasting home!

12. Murder

"I'm blessed a lot", I thought,
"With these gems of mine,
They are with me in my ups and downs
In all the mischiefs we do
I found peace with them
Lived with them most days
Proclaimed to the world about
Those treasures I possessed
For a lifetime ,creating memories,
To cherish forever, till my grave
Friends with the same wavelength, I said
In every worldly matters.

But when on spiritual things I looked,
"We were different", I thought
"Ought to share the good news to them
Lead them to eternity,
Save them from eternal death
Give them the chance to be called
Children of the Most High by Salvation
And the real happiness which I acquired."
So I tried, in my words and deeds
In the least time I spend

To bring them to Joy
And Love and Peace and Spirit.

But they denied, their culture opposed my views
Their worldly desires denied my happiness
Tempted me to do their sins
Forced me to take part in their deeds
And separate me from my Paradise
Teased me for my plans
Bullied me for mine is different
Gradually hatred grew in me,
Thinking : "They will be paid back,
On the day of Judgement
For ignoring the Most High."
Felt happy at their losses,
Thinking : "It is repaid."
Forgiveness didn't I see
Since then, till the Great Day...

***

Waiting for my reward, I stood,
Looking onto white clouds
Before Him, the Mighty One
But He told: "Your name is not seen,
For you are a murderer!"
Startled I : "How come?
Hadn't touched a knife my entire life!"

“Not by deeds, but by thoughts,” He replied
“Hadn’t I commanded you?
For one who hates his brother,
Is a murderer by heart,
He is denied eternal heaven,
Now go, to the fire created for you,
And your ‘gems’ whom you didn’t harvest!”

13. Faith

'Twas all fine until one day
Suddenly something wasn't right
I went to church but in vain
I prayed and prayed but felt like
Those bouncing back from the ceiling
I cried loud but He didn't hear
The world offered nothing either
Messed up everything I tried
Wondered whether He ignored me
Whether He left me without warning
As if God became silent.

Days passed by yet the same
When one day I fell exhausted
'Can't bear it longer', I said
Then I heard His voice,
"Hold onto your faith!
The waves will lash
The storms will rise
Though you cannot see
Though you don't know,
Never lose your faith
Put your trust in Me
Who makes you soar.

I won't turn a blind eye
To all your efforts.
Though you don't find
All the answers to your worries
But always remember that
I'm in control!
I am the same God
Who led you in the past
I'm just preparing you
To trust me in the storm!

14. The stone

I was angry, I was cold
I kept bitterness for long
I couldn’t control my anger
Replayed every little details
Complained every single day
My mind wandered each moment
One minute I’m okay but the next I'm not
Told to myself: “They are worse,
They don’t deserve my forgiveness
Nor do they deserve God's kindness
How can someone hurt others much?
They should be repaid for what they did.”

The weight in me grew harder
Like a very big stone
Sinking deep into my heart
When all at once God said:
"Melt it", I was shocked
"No God," I mumbled,
"I can't and I won't"

And He reached into my soul:
"Why do you even pray?
Why do you go to church?

What's the use of it
If you can't forgive, it's pointless.
What if I kept all your sins?
Hadn't I forgiven whenever you cried?
Likewise you ought to forgive others
Take away the bitterness, the coldness
When you try to melt your stone
That's when the true gospel starts!"

15. All That You Are

Lord, I want to know,
I want to experience
Not only in what I've learned,
Not only in what I've felt so far,
But in all that You are.

I know You as the Almighty,
Faithful and full of love
Creator, powerful and kind,
Eternal, unmatched,
The greatest of all.

Yet I want to know You as a whole
Not just bits and pieces
To be guided by Your voice;
I want to explore the depths of You
And taste and see Your fullness.

For Your ways are higher,
Your thoughts far greater.
You are the storehouse of wisdom
Your greatness beyond my understanding,
Your power beyond measure.

You love us more than we imagine,
You give far more than we deserve.
When everyone fails, You stay
And move the mountains
To provide for your children.

And now when I see You,
Everything else falls into place.
My heart is filled with a peace
That surpasses all understanding,
And I am left gazing
At You and You alone!

16. To Joseph

All you ever did was dream
A dream God placed within your soul
Yet they cast you into a pit
And called it your fate.

You were faithful till the end
Still you ended up in prison
How did you not complain to God
When heaven felt so far away?

Not days, but years you lived in bondage,
Paying for a sin you never committed.
Yet your spirit did not break
Nor your hope grow thin.

How did despair not claim your heart?
If I were there, I surely would have fallen.
Where people complain for the silliest things,
You held onto God's word.

Your faith did not flicker,
Your courage did not fade.
You trusted the God who saw you-

He who put that dream in you.

Where men keep bitterness for ages,
You forgave those who hurt you
Even when they were your own blood
You counted their betrayal a blessing

And so God lifted you in His time.
Like a bough beside the spring
Bearing fruits in every season
As a blessing to your nation.

17. Random Musings - Part 1

" Just that He is listening,
Just that I can sit near Him
And share all my worries
Is more than enough
To bring me peace."

"But as for me,
Christ is my best friend
And it's the only truth
I cherish the most."

"I take rest,
Within the veil of flowers,
Embracing the leaves,
And lying on the grass,
When I raise my eyes above
And thank the Creator
For this Poem of Earth."

18. Random Musings - Part 2

"Our peace doesn't come from
Having all the answers to our worries
But from knowing that
God is in control."

"I'm glad, joy lives in me,
As I'm one of the progeny of Abraham,
One of the million stars in the sky,
That account to his generation."

"And finally on that day,
We the partakers of that one bread,
Can colour our dreams,
Can be free,
Can fly.....!"

19. Guarding the Distance

I watched the sea from afar
To see the silence it reflects
The waves still and calm
The waters clear and bright

Neither the cerulean skies,
Nor the palm tree branches
Fluttered even the slightest,
Like a painting before my eyes.

But, as I walked closer
Musing the broken shells below
Amidst the wet sands filled with
Scribblings of folks all around

All were vanished within seconds
By the waves lashing the shore,
It no longer remained silent,
But roared louder than all

Stillness became hard to find
Calmness taken away by the waters
Too harsh for the ears
And annoying for the mind

Likewise were people, I realized
What I saw them as a painting,
Eventually washes away to become
Just colours on the canvas.

Them those that were calm at first
Were the loudest at the end,
As closer I drew near and tried
To peep into their inner minds.

I finally realized that
Everything is temporary
And it's God and God alone
Who truly matters!

So, as I departed from the seashore,
Bidding goodbye to the loud waves
Likewise I moved farther away
To guard the distance between me and people.

20. Perspective

Since when have we learned
To see things in a different way?
Hasn't time taught us to change
Our perspectives about different things?
Wouldn't we appreciate things
Or ideas that we earlier judged?
Haven't we unlearned few things
Which we earlier thought to be right?
Haven't our experiences taught us that
Certain people are not always right
And anyone can be wrong at any time?
Haven't we learned to look
At our own mistakes and not others' ?
And isn't God the magician,
To help us change our whole self
And look at the world in the most rational way?

21. Pictures

Our lives are governed by pictures,
Pictures of ourselves and others.
From longing to be like others
To showing what we have in ours
Our lives are ruled by
Pictures of people and self.

Things that we don't need,
Pictures tell us to buy them.
Emotions that we needn't express,
Pictures feed their necessity.
Places we needn't go,
Pictures pack our bags to there.

No deaths, only births
No failures, only degrees
No losses, only profits
No storms, only calmness
No sadness, but only happiness
Were bound to appear in those clicks.

Had we known the gloomy faces
Hiding behind their masks
Or the unknown versions hidden

Deep within their bones,
Wouldn't we learn to embrace
Both what we possess,
As well as what we don't?

And then in the stillness,
Where every image fades,
There is the God who sees us
No masks, no screens
He who loved us
With an Unconditional Love,
Embracing our true self
Just as we are!

www.ingramcontent.com/pod-product-compliance
Lightning Source LLC
Chambersburg PA
CBHW070649240926
51846CB00003BA/847
9789375273875

1. मेरी कविताएं

असंख्य वर्षों से कविताएं
उमड़ती है ,मचलती है, छलकती है
डूबती है भावों में,
बहती हैं मेरी आंखों से
शहर के साथ-साथ बदलती हैं
पर हमेशा मेरे साथ चलती हैं।
कभी उग आती है
कैक्टस के कांटों में
कभी ढल जाती है चांदनी रातों में
कभी आंख बचाती हूं इनसे
तो भी आंख मिलाती हैं
मुस्कुरा कर रसोई में
ले जाती हैं
फिर बेली जाती हैं
चकले पर
रोटियों के साथ
तो कभी मांजी जाती हैं
बर्तनों के पास
झाड़ी जाती है अलमारियों की धूल से
फिर वर्षों बाद याद आ जाती हैं भूल से

Acknowledgements

शब्दों के इस आकाश में
जब मैंने अपने मन के पंख फैलाए,
तो हर अनुभव, हर संबंध,
हर स्मृति ने मुझे उड़ान दी।
"नीलपंख" उसी उड़ान का रंगीन विस्तार है—
जहाँ भावनाएँ कविता बनकर झरती हैं,
और सपने गीतों में ढलते हैं।

मैं हृदय से आभार व्यक्त करती हूँ—

* उन अनगिनत क्षणों का, जिनमें जीवन ने मुझे आँसू और हँसी दोनों दिए, ताकि मैं उन्हें कविता में रूपांतरित कर सकूँ।

* जीवन के अभावों,भावनात्मक असुरक्षाओं,वेदनाओं का जिन्होंने मुझे साहस और हिम्मत प्रदान की।

"नीलपंख" मेरे लिए केवल कविताओं का संग्रह नहीं,
यह आत्मा की उड़ान है, भावनाओं का गान है,
और उन सभी का आशीर्वाद है जिन्होंने मुझे शब्दों का आकाश दिया।

कविता केवल लिखी नहीं जाती—
कविता जी जाती है, महसूस की जाती है, और बाँटी जाती है।

पर लोगों की तरह ,
साथ नहीं छोड़ती,
कभी कष्ट में मुंह नहीं मोड़ती।
थाम लेती है मेरा हाथ
क्योंकि
असंख्य वर्षों से कविताएं
उमड़ती है ,मचलती है, छलकती है
डूबती है भावों में,
बहती हैं मेरी आंखों से...।

2. भावी भारत के कर्णधार

भावी भारत के कर्णधार,
देखो समक्ष सफलता अपार,
बन स्व जीवन रथ के संचालक,
दौड़ा दो अश्व निर्मल नील फलक,
ऐसी दहाड़ तुम दिखला दो कि
छा जाओ जग पर बन वज्र प्रहार,
स्व अश्रु आग बनाकर के
तार सप्तक सा झंकार करो,
जागो ,उठो ,वीर बनो,
नव युग का निर्माण करो,
अपने साहस कर्मठता से,
बाधाओं पर वार करो,
डगमग डगमग अपनी नैय्या,
तूफानों से पार करो।
क्षीण,क्षीण,क्षीण से
वीर ,वीर ,वीर तक
स्थूल, स्थूल,स्थूल से
सूक्ष्म, सूक्ष्म ,सूक्ष्म तक
इस भूतल पर
शौर्य अंगार से

हाहाकार करो
मेरे भावी भारत के कर्णधार
अपने साहस, कर्मठता से
नवयुग का निर्माण करो।

3. साथी

जिनसे जी भरकर बातें होती थीं,

अब उनसे बहुत कम मुलाक़ातें होती हैं।

ना बिना मिले शामें ढलती थीं,

अब तन्हाई में ही रातें होती हैं।

वो हँसी, वो चाय के प्याले, वो कहानियाँ,

अब मोहलतों में ही सौगातें होती हैं।

दिल के करीब थे, रूह के साथी थे,

अब ख़्वाबों में ही मुलाक़ातें होती हैं।

शहरों की दूरियों ने रिश्तों को ढक लिया,

अब दुआओं में ही बातें होती हैं।

"नील" कहे, ये फ़ासले भी अजीब हैं,

दूर रहकर भी दिलों की बातें होती हैं।

4. अलविदा दादी...

आपका प्यार , लाड,दुलार,
तीखी सी फटकार,जोर की मार
मेरा बचपन,मेरी कहानी,
मेरा,जीवन,मेरी जवानी
मेरे जज़्बात,मेरे खयालात,
मेरी रगों का खून,मेरी आंखों का पानी,
मेरे सपने,मेरे अपने,
मेरे यार ,मेरे दोस्त,
मेरी चाहत,मेरी दौलत,
मेरी किस्मत,मेरी मोहोब्बत
वो नीम का पेड़,वो घर का आंगन,
वो बालाजी मंदिर
गांव का सरकारी स्कूल,
आपका दिल दुखाने की भूल
वो भेड़ बकरियों के रेवड़ ,
वो बीड के कैर बबूल
वो मेहंदी लगे हाथ,
वो अम्मा जी का साथ
वो गर्म दोपहरी,
आप के साथ वो हिंदी साहित्य की बात

मेरी किताबे,वो घर की दहलीज
और पुराने एल्बमों में दबी हर पल की याद
वो तेरे हाथ का प्रसाद,
वो हर वक्त कानों में गूंजती नीलू नीलू की आवाज
राम स्तुति की हर एक चौपाई,
हम दोनो के साथ की खूबसूरत तन्हाई
वो घर का चौका चूल्हा,
बाड़े में पड़ा पेड़ का झूला
वो सावन के मोर,
तालाब का छोर,घर की छत
परसों से लिखे गए,
तेरे नाम वो कई काल्पनिक खत
व्रत , उपवास,पूजा और पाठ,
ईश्वर पर तेरा अटूट विश्वास
मेरा दिल मेरी धड़कन,
आज तेरे साथ न होने का अहसास
ये नौकरी की मजबूरी,ये मीलों की दूरी
ये मां होने का भाव,
वो मेरा गांव जाने का चाव
वो दिवाली के दिए,
होली रत्जगे के गीत
शंकर के मंदिर की ऊंची घंटी
वो पड़ोस में रहने वाली मेरी सहेली बंटी
वो बयासन माई ,वो लखेरी काकी,
तेरे हाथ की चाकी
उफ्फ.................................
क्या भूलूं क्या याद करूं मैं....?

बस......................................

समझ नहीं आ रहा तेरे बिना कैसे

रहूं मैं....?

5. आईना

कुछ आईने चेहरा नहीं दिखाते
दिखाते हैं कोरा अतीत
जहां धुंधले रंगों में
छुपे होते हैं अधूरे
संवाद।
वह आईने सिर्फ आंखों को नहीं
भीतर की परतों को
टटोलते हैं जैसे कोई पुरानी धुन
जो दिल के किसी कोने से
अचानक गूंज उठती है ।
और तब समझ आता है कि
आईना सिर्फ चमकता नहीं
वह थामता है समय को
जैसे कविता थामती है
एक टूटे हुए मन का सच।

6. पहला पहला मिलना

वो बादलों का घिरना,
वो हवाओं का बहना,
वो बूंदों का बरसना,
वो मेंरी सांसों का महकना
और तेरे दिल का ज़ोर से धड़कना
उफ्फ, वो हमारा
पहला पहला मिलना
सच में बहुत याद आता है।
तुझे अपने इतना करीब पाकर
खुद से इतना दूर निकल जाना
उस हल्की ठंड,
भीगे मौसम में
हम दोनों का
सिहर जाना
उफ्फ,वो हमारा
पहला पहला मिलना
सच में बहुत याद आता है।

7. मन की बात

अक्सर हम यह करते हैं
इससे बात,
उससे बात
इसकी बात,
उसकी बात
पर जो नहीं करते
वह है –
सीधी बात,
सही बात,
सच्ची बात,
मन की बात।

8. जिनके मायके नहीं होते हैं....

कितनी खुशकिस्मत होती होंगी वो लड़कियां
जिनके अपने मायके होते हैं....
जहां जाते ही सारी यादें और बचपन के वही पुराने जायके होते है...
जहां करता है
तुम्हारा कोई हर साल इंतज़ार
कि कब आओगी....?
कब दिल की सारी बातें बताकर
अपने तन और मन की थकान मिटाओगी.....
देखो....
ये गलियां तुम्हारी राह तकती हैं ...
आज भी तुम्हारी यादें ,बातें
घर के कोने-कोने में धड़कती है...
जहां हैं ऐसे अपने जो सिर्फ सुनेंगे नहीं....
सच में...हां,हां बिल्कुल सच में
समझेंगे तुम्हारे जज्बात
जहां ना बात बात में देनी पड़ेगी तुम्हे कोई सफाई
यहां हैं ,बुआ,
पर दादा,परदादी,चाचा ,चाची,
पापा और सबसे प्यारी माई....
कुछ घर सिर्फ घर नहीं होते

पूरा युग होते हैं
जो कैद कर लेते है आपकी आत्मा
और फिर कभी आजाद नहीं करते उसे...
चाहे आप दुनिया के किसी कोने में चले जाएं
या पता नहीं ?
आप आजाद होना नहीं चाहते
कुछ आकृतियां जहन में ऐसी जज़्ब हो चुकी है कि
उन्हें विस्मृत कर पाना ...
कम से कम इस जन्म में तो असंभव है।

9. आत्मा की चीख

क्या आपको पता है ?
कि समय के साथ
आत्मा के छिलके भी उतरते हैं
छितरा जाते हैं
बस यूं ही जमीन पर
कभी इनमें से खून रिसता है
कभी यूं ही निकलते हैं आंसू भी
पर ताज्जुब इस बात का है कि
जब वह छितरा जाते हैं
दिखते किसी को नहीं
ना ही चुभते हैं किसी के पैर में भी
बस रह जाते हैं मौन की तरह
जो चीखता है भीतर
पर सुनाई नहीं देता बाहर
और तब हम मुस्कुराते हैं
जैसे -
कुछ हुआ ही नहीं
पर भीतर ?
एक पूरा मौसम बदल चुका होता है ।

10. स्पष्टवादी

सुनो.... मैं स्पष्टवादी हूं।
मेरी विशेषता है कि
मैं साफ-साफ बोलता हूं
हर किसी को
अलग-अलग लहजों से तोलता हूं
मैं किसी का दिल नहीं दुखाता
ना ही लोगों को मैं बार-बार मानता
भाई ...
बोलोगे नहीं तो जीतोगे कैसे ?
सच बताओ चुप रहने वालों को...
पूछता कौन है वैसे?
पर मै कहती हूँ
लेकिन स्पष्ट वादी जी...
क्या आपको कभी-कभी साफ-साफ बोलने के बाद
अपने तीखे शब्दों में व्यक्ति को तोलाने के बाद
उन्हें हर वक्त आईना दिखाने पर
फिर मझधार में छोड़कर
यूं ही मुंह मोड़ कर गुजर जाने पर
कभी अफसोस नहीं होता?
कि तुम्हारे साफ बोलने के खौफनाक अंदाज़ ने

उसके व्यक्तित्व को तार तार करने के प्रयास ने
ला दिया है उसे सीधे स्वर्ग से नरक के द्वार पर
घसीट कर पहुंचा दिया है तुमने .....
हां ....हां तुमने
शर शय्या पर I
जहां तुम्हारे व्यंग्य बाण बार-बार उसे चुभते हैं
हृदय उसका लहूलुहान , बिलबिलाता है
कुछ दिनों तक बेचारा वह स्वयं को भी भूल जाता है
वैसे स्पष्टवादी जी
अविस्मरणीय योगदान है आपका
देश के विकास में
गौर से देखिए मित्रों...
ऐसे स्पष्टवादी असंख्य यमराज हैं
आज हमारे आसपास में।

11. अंतहीन सफर

कुछ यात्राएं ऐसी होती हैं
जिनका प्रारंभ तो होता है
पर अंत नहीं होता ।

ना ही होता कोई परिणाम
उनके नसीब में होता है सफर
एक अंतहीन सफर,
जो बिना नक्शे, बिना ठिकाने
लगातार चलता है।

कभी धूप सी तपिश,
कभी छांव सा सुकून,
कभी खुद से मुलाकात,
कभी खुद से मुलाकात का जुनून।

कभी लगता सफर है जीवन,
मंजिलें तो बस भ्रम हैं,
जो मिल जाएँ तो भी अधूरी,
जो ना मिलें तो भी पूरी।

तो चलिए, चलते रहें
इस अनंत यात्रा में,
जहाँ हर क्षण , प्रत्येक को
धकेल रहा है
जीवन की अंतिम यात्रा की ओर।

12. बिन बाप की बेटी

अपनी थकान कहां जताती होगी
बिन बाप की बेटी
किसे हर दर्द बताती होगी।
किस से कहती होगी गुड़िया लाना पापा
किसे अपनी सहेलियों के
किस्से सुनाती होगी
बिन बाप की बेटी किसे हर दर्द बताती होगी?

स्कूल में सबके पापा देखकर,
निश्छल मुस्कान में
अपना खालीपन छुपाती होगी
उसकी बढ़ती उम्र,
घरवालों की परेशानी बन जाती होगी
बिन बाप की बेटी किसे हर दर्द बताती होगी?

जीवन की कठिन परीक्षाओं में,
जब वो घबराती होगी,
चल कर गिरना,गिरकर उठना
जब अपने आप सीख जाती होगी
आख़िर अपने घाव किसे दिखाती होगी?

बिन बाप की बेटी किसे हर दर्द बताती होगी?

परिस्थितियों से लड़कर,
जीवन में आगे बढ़कर
जब पराए घर जाती होगी
किस के सीने में छुपकर अमूल्य अश्रु बहाती होगी
बिन बाप की बेटी किसे हर दर्द बताती होगी।

13. ज़रूरी है...

सारे दिन का जीया हुआ,
किसी एक को बताना जरूरी है।
जवानी का एक दिन कैसा खोया,
ये किसी एक को समझाना जरूरी है।

ये दफ्तर,ये दुनिया,
ये इश्क में हारे हुए लोग..
रोज शाम किसी एक को ,
जिंदा भी नजर आना जरूरी है।

हर किसी को नसीब कहां 'वो' एक शख्स
पर जीने के लिए इस तरह,
करीब जाना जरूरी है ।
डूबते सूरज के साथ,
डूबती उम्मीदों को
फिर हर सुबह समंदर से किनारे लाना जरूरी है

मौत के ख्याल,बच्चों के सवाल,
इन सभी के लिए लौटकर घर जाना जरूरी है ,
भटकते बादलों को,

किसी सहरा पर बरसाना जरूरी है
अपनी जवानी बेचकर तेरा मुस्कुराना जरूरी है

जवानी का एक दिन कैसे खोया,
किसी एक को सुनाना जरूरी है।
सारे दिन का जीया हुआ,
किसी एक को बताना जरूरी है।

14. महकता गुलाब

मेरी आंखों का
अधूरा मुकम्मल ख्वाब था ।
वो लडका नहीं ,
महकता गुलाब था।
मोहब्बत का समन्दर
बेशकीमती यादों का बवंडर
मेरी तन्हा रातों का,
चमकता आफताब था
वो लडका नहीं
महकता गुलाब था।
मेरे दिल का शहजादा,
मुझ में कहीं मुझ से ज्यादा,
मेरी जिंदगी के रहस्यों की
बंद किताब था,
वो लडका नहीं
महकता गुलाब था।

15. म से मां

मां मैं अब जानती हूं
कि मां होना
इतना आसान नहीं होता
एक मां होने के लिए
अपने शौक, इच्छाएं, सपने, उम्मीदें
सबको
भाड़ में झोंकना पड़ता है
अपने मन में उमडते
भावनाओं के ज्वार को
ममता की नदी में
ठंडा करना पड़ता है
मां मैं जानती हूं कि
मां होना इतना आसान नहीं होता
जाने कितनी बार
अकेले ग़लतियां कर करके
सीखना पड़ता है
जाने कितनी रातें.
सिर्फ खुद से ही करके बातें
काटनी पड़ती है
दुनिया के ताने, अपनों की हकीकतें

जानते हुए भी,
सच कहने से रो-रो कर
खुद को रोकना पड़ता है
'तुम तो मां हो
अपने बच्चों के लिए इतना तो
करना ही पड़ता है'
ऐसी बातें
जाने कितने कर्तव्यविमुख
लोगों से सुननी पड़ती हैं
दर्द का घूंट पी पीकर,
अपने दूध और रक्त से
सींच सींच कर
संतान को पालना पड़ता है
मां मैं जानती हूं
अब कि मां होना इतना
आसान नहीं होता
आत्मनिर्भर बनने की होड़ में,
आधुनिकता की इस दौड़ में,
बच्चों को गले लगाने के लिए
एक कौर अपने हाथ से खिलाने के लिए
हडबडाते हुए पर्स उठाकर
सीधे घर दौड़ना पड़ता है
मां मैं अब सच में जानती हूं
कि मां होना इतना आसान नहीं होता।

16. अनकहे अहसास

तेरी आँखों के चढ़ते-उतरते नूर से,
मैंने अपना मिज़ाज बदलते देखा है।

तेरी आवारगी और तेरी बेबाकियों को,
धीरे-धीरे खामोशियों में ढलते देखा है।

शफ़्फ़ाफ़ वजूद रखता था जो शख़्स कभी,
कड़कती धूप में उसे छाँव को तरसते देखा है।

वैसे तो कोई ख़ास ताल्लुक नहीं है तेरा-मेरा,
फिर भी तेरे अहसासों को क़रीब से गुजरते देखा है।

वक़्त बीत जाने पर बेमानी हो जाती हैं कुछ बातें,
लम्हों को अभी से फिर कभी नहीं में बदलते देखा है।

कभी तो भरोसा कर साफ़-दिल राहगीरों पर,
'नील' ने राहगीरों को ज़िंदगी से गुजरते देखा है।

17. प्रेम

प्रेम कोई शब्द नहीं, यह तो आत्मा की धड़कन है,
हर सांस में छुपकर जीवन को देता स्पंदन है।

प्रेम वह रोशनी है, जो अंधेरों में राह दिखाता है,
प्रेम वह स्पर्श है, जो टूटे दिल को जोड़ जाता है।

प्रेम वह नज़र है, जिसमें हजारों कहानियाँ छुपी हैं,
प्रेम वह मुस्कान है, जो हर दर्द को सहला जाती है।

प्रेम वह विश्वास है, जो दूरी में भी पास कराता है,
प्रेम वह गीत है, जो खामोशियों में भी गूंजता है।

प्रेम कोई बंधन नहीं, यह तो मुक्त आकाश है,
जहाँ दो आत्माएँ मिलकर अनंत यात्रा पर निकलती हैं।

18. जीवनसाथी

तू मेरे जीवन का सबसे अनमोल सहारा है,
हर कठिन राह पर साथ खड़ा उजियारा है।

तेरे संग मुस्कानें भी और आँसू भी बाँटे हैं,
तेरे संग ही सपनों के रंग हमने छाँटे हैं।

जब थक कर गिरने लगती है मेरी हिम्मत,
तेरी आँखों में मिलता फिर से साहस है।

जीवनसाथी केवल नाम नहीं, यह तो आत्मा का मेल है,
तेरे संग हर पल जीना ही मेरा रोचक खेल है।

तू ही मेरी सबसे सच्ची पहचान है,
तेरे बिना अधूरी हूँ मैं, तू ही मेरी जान है।

www.ingramcontent.com/pod-product-compliance
Lightning Source LLC
Chambersburg PA
CBHW070652240926
51846CB00003BA/889
9789375270010